LIFE CYCLE OF A PIG

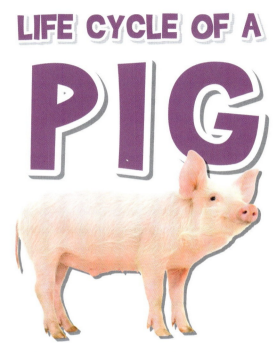

by Noah Leatherland

Minneapolis, Minnesota

Credits

All images are courtesy of Shutterstock.com, unless otherwise specified. With thanks to Getty Imag⟨ Photo, and iStockphoto. Cover – tanyaya, YummyBuum, Ekaterina_Mikhaylova, Sonechko57, Boroc Tsekhmister. Recurring images – Voin_Sveta, uiliaaa, YummyBuum, Terdpong, tanyaya. 2 – Tsekhm ArtbyPixel, Irina Kozorog. 4 – Monkey Business Images, vic josh, Prostock-studio. 5 – Dernkadel, G mimagephotography, wavebreakmedia. 6 – Julia Lototskaya. 7 – ArtbyPixel. 8 – Aksenova Nata 10 – Foto-Sabine. 11 – Oleksandr Khokhlyuk. 12 – Alexwilko, Maleo. 13 – Thuwanan Krueabudd 15 – Helga Chirk. 16 – Bogdan Cherniak. 17 – grandbrothers. 18 – Frank Cornelissen. 19 – Nata, Opiyo, Laurie E Wilson, Borodatch. 21 – ABWitzPix089. 22 – LittlePerfectStock, ArtbyPixel. 23

Library of Congress Cataloging-in-Publication Data is available at www.loc.gov or upon request from the publisher.

ISBN: 979-8-88916-960-4 (hardcover)
ISBN: 979-8-89232-488-5 (paperback)
ISBN: 979-8-89232-124-2 (ebook)

© 2025 BookLife Publishing
This edition is published by arrangement with BookLife Publishing.

North American adaptations © 2025 Bearport Publishing Company. All rights reserved. No part of this publication may be reproduced in whole or in part, stored in any retrieval system, or transmitted in any form or by any means, electronic, mechanical, photocopying, recording, or otherwise, without written permission from the publisher. Bearport Publishing is c division of Chrysalis Education Group.

For more information, write to Bearport Publishing, 5357 Penn Avenue South, Minneapolis, MN 55419.

Contents

What Is a Life Cycle?. 4
Pigs on the Farm. 6
Getting Ready for Piglets 8
Playful Piglets 10
Mother's Milk 12
Noisy Oinks 14
Leaving the Litter 16
All Grown Up 18
The End of Life. 20
Life Cycle of a Pig. 22
Glossary 24
Index 24

WHAT IS A LIFE CYCLE?

All living things go through different stages of life. We come into the world and grow over time. Eventually, we die. This is the life cycle.

BABY

TODDLER

CHILD

As humans, we start life as babies. We grow into toddlers and children. Then, we become teenagers. Finally, we are adults and get even older. We may have babies of our own, and then the cycle begins again.

PIGS ON THE FARM

Animals on the farm go through life cycles, too. Farm pigs are **domestic** animals. This means they are not wild. People keep them as **livestock**.

There are many different **breeds** of pigs. They are all different colors and sizes.

A group of pigs is sometimes called a drove.

Some farms have only a few pigs, while others have hundreds or thousands. Farmers raise these animals for their meat.

GETTING READY FOR PIGLETS

Female pigs can have babies. A **pregnant** pig grows babies inside her body. After about four months, the babies are ready to be born.

A PREGNANT PIG

A female pig that has not yet had babies is called a gilt.

A few days before she is ready to give **birth**, the mother pig makes a nest out of straw. Then, she gives birth to about 10 babies called piglets. This is her litter.

PLAYFUL PIGLETS

Many newborn piglets can walk within the first few days of their lives. Some even run and jump on their first day.

A newborn piglet weighs about 2 pounds (1.4 kg).

Piglets have a hard time keeping themselves warm. They often stay close to their mother to get heat from her body. Sometimes, farmers help keep piglets warm by giving them blankets and heat lamps.

MOTHER'S MILK

Piglets need their mother's milk to have a healthy start to life. They get **nutrients** from this milk.

Piglets grow quickly! They double their birth weight in their first week.

A TEAT

The little pigs start drinking soon after they are born. They get milk from a row of **teats** on their mother's body. By the time they are one week old, each piglet will have chosen a teat that they drink from each time.

NOISY OINKS

Pigs young and old make lots of different sounds. They can grunt, oink, and squeal to talk to one another.

Pigs make different sounds if they are happy or scared.

A mother pig will make noises to tell her babies it's time to drink. Piglets can tell the difference between sounds their mother makes and those from another pig.

LEAVING THE LITTER

For the first few weeks, piglets stay close to their mother and drink her milk. They start to wander farther away from her as they get older. After about a month, the piglets start eating solid food.

Pigs eat different types of food, but they munch mostly on a mix of corn and soybeans.

Pigs in groups often learn from one another.

Piglets have close bonds with their brothers and sisters as they grow up. They may form groups with piglets from other litters, too.

ALL GROWN UP

When they are about a year and a half old, the pigs become adults. Adult pigs are very large. For some breeds, fully grown pigs can weigh more than 660 lb. (300 kg).

Pigs have a great sense of smell! Some pigs help humans find mushrooms underground.

A **male** pig is called a boar when it's about six months old. A female pig of the same age can have piglets of her own. The mother pig is called a sow after she's had her first litter.

THE END OF LIFE

There are very few **predators** that hunt adult pigs. But some animals will try to eat piglets. Farmers have to be careful to keep piglets safe on their farms.

A BOBCAT

A COYOTE

Bobcats and coyotes are some of the animals that hunt piglets.

Pigs can live for about 20 years. However, most farm pigs don't live this long since they are raised for their meat.

LIFE CYCLE OF A PIG

A pig starts its life as a piglet. Its mother keeps it warm. The piglet drinks its mother's milk and grows bigger and bigger each day. Eventually, it becomes an adult.

PIGLET

ADULT PIG

During its life, a pig may give birth to piglets of its own. Eventually, the pig will die, but the piglets live on and have even more pigs. This keeps the life cycle going!

Glossary

birth when a female has a baby

breeds different types of an animal

domestic tamed for use by humans

female a pig that can give birth to young

livestock animals that are raised by people on farms or ranches

male a pig that cannot give birth to young

nutrients substances needed by plants and animals to grow and stay healthy

predators animals that hunt and eat other animals

pregnant when a female animal has babies growing inside her

teats parts of a mother pig's body where milk comes from

Index

breeds 6, 18
domestic 6
farmers 7, 11, 20
litter 9, 16–17, 19
milk 12–13, 16, 22
nest 9
noise 15
predators 20
teats 13
warm 11, 22